# THINKING, MAKING DECISIONS AND SOLVING PROBLEMS

By

Prof HOWDY KAHNENMA

# TABLE OF CONTENTS

# INTRODUCTION

## THINKING

The act of creating thoughts with one's mind

## CRITICAL THINKING

The goal of education is widely accepted to be critical thinking. The definitions of it are disputed, but they can be understood as different interpretations of the same fundamental idea: careful thinking with a goal in mind. The scope of such thinking, the kind of goal, the criteria and standards for thoughtful thinking, and the thinking components on which they focus are all different in concepts. Respect for students' autonomy and preparing them for success in life and democratic citizenship have been cited as reasons for its adoption as an educational objective. People who are "critical thinkers" have the attitudes and skills to think critically when needed. The abilities can be directly identified; the dispositions indirectly by thinking about what factors make it easier or harder to use the abilities. To determine the extent to which a person possesses such dispositions and abilities, standardized tests have been developed. They have improved experimentally as a result of educational intervention, particularly when it includes mentoring, anchored instruction, and dialogue. The relationship between critical thinking and other types of thinking, the alleged bias in critical thinking theories and instruction, and the generalizability of critical thinking across domains have all sparked debate.

Employers in a variety of industries look for candidates who possess the skills of problem-solving and decision-making, which are similar but distinct. Skills that can improve your value as an employee and possibly increase your chances of landing a job are the ability to approach and resolve workplace issues. Understanding how they differ and how to develop them can help you work more effectively and independently if you want to learn how to improve your problem-solving and decision-making skills at work.

This article compares decision-making and problem-solving skills, explains how to use them at work, and offers advice on how to improve your skills.

Get the most recent news about the hottest topics, career advice, and more!

# CHAPTER 1

# PROBLEM-SOLVING VS. DECISION-MAKING

## PROBLEM-SOLVING

It is an analytical approach to finding possible solutions to a problem. The process is complicated, and judgment calls or choices may need to be made along the way. Finding the best solution is the primary objective. Problem-solving involves identifying a problem, determining its causes, asking probing questions, and coming up with potential solutions. The solution is easier to see when more information is gathered.

## DECISION-MAKING

It is the process of selecting a solution based on your judgment, the situation, the facts, your knowledge, or a combination of the data that are available. The objective is to steer clear of potential problems. An important part of making decisions is recognizing opportunities. Decision-making is frequently a component of problem-solving.

# WHY PROBLEM-SOLVING AND DECISION-MAKING ARE IMPORTANT

Skills like problem-solving and decision-making are crucial because they can assist you in navigating a variety of workplace scenarios. They work well together and can deal with many of the same problems. Critical thinking is required for both decision-making and problem-solving. All careers and industries require decision-making and problem-solving skills. Employers typically place a high value on these abilities in applicants for jobs because they can assist businesses in resolving complex issues and situations. They demonstrate your capacity to consider a variety of scenarios and arrive at well-informed choices that are beneficial to the business.

A company may, for instance, have a number of issues that all necessitate time and resources. A decent supervisor or pioneer can choose which issues to focus on. As part of the problem-solving process, this includes making a lot of decisions and carrying out the steps to fix the problem.

# HOW TO USE PROBLEM-SOLVING AND DECISION-MAKING SKILLS

To work on your productivity at work, you can follow a smoothed out and coordinated way to deal with tackle issues and decide. To get the most out of your ability to solve problems and make decisions, follow these five steps:

1. Define the issue

Determining the issue or problem is the first step. Analyze the issue and consider its possible causes once you have identified it. Make an effort to locate any sub problems within the larger issue. Before beginning to consider potential decisions and solutions, it is essential to comprehend the issue. Having a problem that is clearly defined can make it easier to make decisions later on. Make your problem as clear as possible by defining or stating it in the most specific terms possible. You could ask yourself these questions to figure out what the problem requires:

• What are the contributing factors to this problem?

• Who are the individuals involved in the problem?

• When does this problem occur?

• Where is this problem occurring?

Before proceeding with the creation of a solution, these questions can clarify relevant information to assist you and others in fully comprehending the issue.

2. Brainstorm different approaches

After defining and analyzing the problem, you can start thinking of different ways to solve it. Try to get feedback from mentors and other people who are involved with the issue in order to get a complete picture of the issue. You can also consider how you have dealt with similar issues in the past. Make sure to take into account both short-term and long-term solutions to the problem. Additionally, consider how potential approaches relate to the objectives and mission of your business.

You can brainstorm alone or with others, and you can use a whiteboard or online software to show what you're thinking. Some common methods for brainstorming are:

• Mental maps: Mind mapping is the process of creating hierarchical illustrations of ideas. Mind maps are useful for problem-solving and decision-making because they can illustrate the connections between various aspects of an issue.

• The SWOT analysis A SWOT analysis can be used to identify a problem's strengths, weaknesses, opportunities, and threats. You can come up with potential solutions if you know these important parts.

• Diagrams: When planning a procedure to address a problem, flowcharts can be helpful because they can be used to illustrate processes and workflows. You can organize your thoughts and design step-by-step solutions to problems by creating a flowchart.

• Rapid genesis: In rapid ideation, everyone involved in a problem writes down as many possible solutions as they can think of in a short amount of time. You can review the ideas as a group after everyone has written them down.

3. Evaluate different approaches

After coming up with ideas, it's time to evaluate them. Consider the advantages and disadvantages of each option, as well as how they would affect your business. Consider the various resources that each decision would necessitate. Taking into account all of these aspects can help you make the best choice for your business..

4. Make your decision

It's time to choose after weighing the pros and cons of each option. You can select from the following decision-making structures:

• Making decisions together: Various points of view contribute to this structure for making decisions.

• Making decisions in command: This structure allows you to make a decision without receiving feedback from others, which may be the quickest method of decision-making.

• Vote-based decisions: With this structure for making decisions, you can quickly get input from many people. People are able to cast votes on a choice from a list of options.

• Making decisions based on consensus: Everyone involved in this structure tries to come to an agreement on a decision. If you want to ensure that your decision has complete support and is not time-sensitive, this process is best because it can be time-consuming.

Ensure that your decision addresses the issue completely and does not exacerbate it. Check to see that the decision is one that your company can actually put into action and is in line with its mission, vision, and core values.

## 5. Implement your decision

After you've made your decision, you can decide how to implement it. Start by identifying primary objectives and deliverables and creating deadlines. Then, outline specific steps to meet the objectives. In the implementation plan, you can include those who are involved with the issue and assign responsibilities to the employees. Then, share your plan with everyone involved with the issue and get feedback.

## 6. Monitor your progress

Once your plan is in place, be sure to monitor your progress. Determine whether you've met your plan's objectives. You can also get feedback from those involved or collect data to gauge the effectiveness of your decision. Adjust your plan if needed, or return to your brainstorm of potential solutions if a new decision is required.

# CHAPTER 2

# PROBLEM-SOLVING AND DECISION-MAKING TIPS

Here are some tips for solving problems and making decisions:

# DEVELOP RELATED SKILLS

You can improve your ability to solve problems and make decisions by learning related skills. The following are some useful skills to learn:

• Thinking analytically: Analytical thinking can assist you in identifying the issue's underlying causes and the best course of action.

• Originality: Your ability to think creatively can help you come up with innovative ideas and make decisions that will benefit your company.

• Analytical reasoning: In order to make the best decision, critical thinking can help you effectively comprehend and analyze an issue.

# COMMUNICATE WITH OTHER PEOPLE

Communication can be key to making excellent decisions. You can ask for feedback from people involved with an issue or ask a mentor for advice. Communicating with other people can help you see different perspectives, which can help you make the best decision possible. You can also ask your colleagues or supervisor how they deal with similar issues to get insight into how other people in your industry decide and solve problems.

# REFLECT ON YOUR PAST DECISIONS

If you want to get better at problem-solving and decision-making, it can be helpful to think back on your previous choices and solutions. Consider your past choices and how successful they were. Take into account the method you used to arrive at a decision and select the elements that proved effective to incorporate into your new approach to problem-solving and decision-making.

# LEARN MORE ABOUT YOUR INDUSTRY

You can better understand various situations and make the best decisions for your business by learning more about your industry. Training, certifications, and courses can help you learn more about your field, and speaking with a mentor can also give you insight into your field.

# RESEARCH OTHER TECHNIQUES

You can also investigate various methods and activities that can assist you in making decisions and resolving issues. You could, for instance, investigate how a respected company solves problems and makes decisions. If you want to make the best decisions for your business, this can help you come up with novel and creative solutions.

# CHAPTER 3

# PROBLEM SOLVING VS DECISION MAKING – WHAT IS THE DIFFERENCE?

The primary distinction between problem-solving and decision-making is that problem-solving is a process, whereas decision-making is an action based on insights gained during the process. The terms "problem solving" and "decision making" are often used interchangeably, but they are not the same thing.

## PROBLEM SOLVING VS DECISION MAKING

Problem solving is a method used to analyze a situation to determine potential solutions. Decision-making is a component of problem solving. The process of solving problems is complicated, and judgment calls—also known as decisions—will need to be made along the way.

Decision making is a decision based on one's judgment. Leaders and managers especially need to have the ability to make sound decisions. As part of the process of finding solutions to problems, you might have to make a lot of choices. Naturally, leaders and managers will need to be able to make decisions in order to choose the best course of action. In most cases, they will also need to confirm the problem and take the next steps to fix it.

# PROBLEM SOLVING OR DECISION MAKING – WHICH IS MOST IMPORTANT?

Although problem-solving and decision-making go hand in hand, they are not mutually exclusive. Leaders and managers need to know the difference between the two and work to improve both skillsets throughout their lives.

When multiple opportunities for action arise, decisions are made. You are able to make choices, but you can't solve the problem.

You can be good at solving problems or finding the cause of a problem, but you won't be able to choose and take actionable next steps to get a good result.

Best-case outcomes are not always the result of quick decisions. When it comes to problem-solving, a strict approach overlooks the fact that a company may need to make the best decision possible given the circumstances (such as constraints on resources, time, and budget).

# HOW DOES PROBLEM SOLVING INVOLVE DECISION MAKING?

The process of solving problems involves making choices. A company may have a number of issues that all require time and resources. Choosing which issue to prioritize is an essential part of management and leadership positions.

## Decision making in 3 steps:

1 Utilize problem-solving techniques to identify potential solutions. This may necessitate making decisions, such as deciding to hold meetings with stakeholders or

appointing team members to address specific problem areas

2. Determine which approach is most appropriate for the issue at hand.

3. Identify the next steps necessary to implement the selected solution.

# THE SIMILARITIES BETWEEN PROBLEM SOLVING AND DECISION MAKING

Although the skills of problem-solving and decision-making are not synonymous, they are both essential for leaders. Because they share some characteristics, the terms "problem solving" and "decision making" are frequently used interchangeably.

**Both problem solving and decision making involve critical thinking.**

In order to choose the next course of action for resolving a problem, critical thinking is the process of challenging not only one's own assumptions but also those of others. Using a combination of research, analysis, questioning, and new idea exploration to gain deep insight into a situation and become informed in a way that isn't limited by peers' subjective perspectives or the status quo is typical of critical thinking..

# CHAPTER 4

# HOW TO USE DECISION MAKING IN SOLVING PROBLEMS

One thing unifies everything: When confronted with a challenge, break it down into manageable parts that necessitate decision-making.

## THE GULF BETWEEN THOSE EMBRACING CHANGE AND THOSE FALLING BEHIND IS GROWING.

Since 2004, Changeboard and Future Talent have provided information and insights on how to cope with change. We are giving you the chance to learn the skills, behaviors, and mindset you need to survive and eventually thrive as we enter an unprecedented disruption period.

# DECISION-MAKING AND PROBLEM-SOLVING

Appreciate the Complexities Involved in Decision-Making & Problem Solving

- Develop evidence to support views
- Analyze situations carefully
- Discuss subjects in an organized way
- Predict the consequences of actions
- Weigh alternatives
- Generate and organize ideas
- Form and apply concepts
- Design systematic plans of action

## A 5-Step Problem-Solving Strategy

1. Specify the problem – a first step to solving a problem is to identify it as specifically as possible.

It involves evaluating the present state and determining how it differs from the goal state.

2. Analyze the problem – analyzing the problem involves learning as much as you can about it. It may be necessary to look beyond the obvious, surface situation, to stretch your imagination and reach for more creative options.

   - seek other perspectives
   - be flexible in your analysis
   - consider various strands of impact
   - brainstorm about all possibilities and implications
   - research problems for which you lack complete information. Get help.

3. **Formulate possible solutions – identify a wide**

   range of possible solutions.

   - try to think of all possible solutions
   - be creative

- consider similar problems and how you have solved them

4. Evaluate possible solutions – weigh the advantages and disadvantages of each solution. Think through each solution and consider how, when, and where you could accomplish each. Consider both immediate and long-term results. Mapping your solutions can be helpful at this stage.

5. Choose a solution – consider 3 factors:
   - compatibility with your priorities
   - amount of risk
   - practicality

## Keys to Problem Solving

- Think aloud – problem solving is a cognitive, mental process. Thinking aloud or talking yourself through the steps of problem solving is useful. Hearing yourself think can facilitate the process.

- Allow time for ideas to "gel" or consolidate. If time permits, give yourself time for solutions to develop. Distance from a problem can allow you to clear your mind and get a new perspective.

- Talk about the problem – describing the problem to someone else and talking about it can often make a problem become more clear and defined so that a new solution will surface.

## Decision Making Strategies

Decision making is a process of identifying and evaluating choices. We make numerous decisions every day and our decisions may range from routine, every-day types of decisions to those decisions which will have far reaching impacts. The types of decisions we make are routine, impulsive, and reasoned. Deciding what to eat for breakfast is a routine decision; deciding to do or buy something at the last minute is considered an impulsive decision; and choosing your college major is, hopefully, a reasoned decision. College coursework often requires you to make the latter, or reasoned decisions.

Decision making has much in common with problem solving. In problem solving you identify and evaluate solution paths; in decision making you make a similar discovery and evaluation of alternatives. The crux of decision making, then, is the careful identification and evaluation of alternatives. As you weigh alternatives, use the following suggestions:

- Consider the outcome each is likely to produce, in both the short term and the long term.
- Compare alternatives based on how easily you can accomplish each.
- Evaluate possible negative side effects each may produce.
- Consider the risk involved in each.
- Be creative, original; don't eliminate alternatives because you have not heard or used them before.

An important part of decision making is to predict both short-term and long-term outcomes for each alternative. You may find that while an alternative seems most desirable at the present, it may pose problems or complications over a longer time period.

# CHAPTER 5

# EFFECTIVE PROBLEM SOLVING AND DECISION MAKING

## TYPES OF DECISION MAKERS

Problem solving and decision making belong together. You cannot solve a problem without making a decision. There are two main types of decision makers. Some people use a systematic, rational approach. Others are more intuitive. They go with their emotions or a gut feeling about the right approach. They may have highly creative ways to address the problem, but cannot explain why they have chosen this approach.

# SIX PROBLEM-SOLVING STEPS

The most effective method uses both rational and intuitive or creative approaches. There are six steps in the process:

1. Identify the problem
2. Search for alternatives
3. Weigh the alternatives
4. Make a choice
5. Implement the choice
6. Evaluate the results and, if necessary, start the process again

# IDENTIFY THE PROBLEM

To solve a problem, you must first determine what the problem actually is. You may think you know, but you need to check it out. Sometimes, it is easy to focus on symptoms, not causes. You use a rational approach to determine what the problem is. The questions you might ask include:

- What have I (or others) observed?
- What was I (or others) doing at the time the problem occurred?
- Is this a problem in itself or a symptom of a deeper, underlying problem?
- What information do I need?
- What have we already tried to address this problem?

For example, the apprentice you supervise comes to you saying that the electric warming oven is not working properly. Before you call a repair technician, you may want to ask a few questions. You may want to find out what the apprentice means by "not working properly." Does he or she know how to operate the equipment? Did he or she check that the equipment was plugged in? Was the fuse or circuit breaker checked? When did it last work?

You may be able to avoid an expensive service call. At the very least, you will be able to provide valuable information to the repair technician that aids in the troubleshooting process.

Of course, many of the problems that you will face in the kitchen are much more complex than a malfunctioning oven. You may have to deal with problems such as:

- Discrepancies between actual and expected food costs
- Labour costs that have to be reduced
- Lack of budget to complete needed renovations in the kitchen
- Disputes between staff

However, the basic problem-solving process remains the same even if the problems identified differ. In fact, the more complex the problem is, the more important it is to be methodical in your problem-solving approach.

# SEARCH FOR ALTERNATIVES

It may seem obvious what you have to do to address the problem. Occasionally, this is true, but most times, it is important to identify possible alternatives. This is where the creative side of problem solving really comes in.

Brainstorming with a group can be an excellent tool for identifying potential alternatives. Think of as many possibilities as possible. Write down these ideas, even if they seem somewhat zany or offbeat on first impression. Sometimes really silly ideas can contain the germ of a superb solution. Too often, people move too quickly into making a choice without really considering all of the options. Spending more time searching for alternatives and weighing their consequences can really pay off.

# WEIGH THE ALTERNATIVES

Once a number of ideas have been generated, you need to assess each of them to see how effective they might be in addressing the problem. Consider the following factors:

- Impact on the organization
- Effect on public relations
- Impact on employees and organizational climate
- Cost
- Legality
- Ethics of actions
- Whether this course is permitted under collective agreements
- Whether this idea can be used to build on another idea

# MAKE A CHOICE

Some individuals and groups avoid making decisions. Not making a decision is in itself a decision. By postponing a decision, you may eliminate a number of options and alternatives. You lose control over the situation. In some cases, a problem can escalate if it is not dealt with promptly. For example, if you do not handle customer complaints promptly, the customer is likely to become even more annoyed. You will have to work much harder to get a satisfactory solution.

# IMPLEMENT THE DECISION

Once you have made a decision, it must be implemented. With major decisions, this may involve detailed planning to ensure that all parts of the operation are informed of their part in the change. The kitchen may need a redesign and new equipment. Employees may need additional training. You may have to plan for a short-term closure while the necessary changes are being made. You will have to inform your customers of the closure.

# EVALUATE THE OUTCOME

Whenever you have implemented a decision, you need to evaluate the results. The outcomes may give valuable advice about the decision-making process, the appropriateness of the choice, and the implementation process itself. This information will be useful in improving the company's response the next time a similar decision has to be made.

# CREATIVE THINKING

Your creative side is most useful in identifying new or unusual alternatives. Too often, you can get stuck in a pattern of thinking that has been successful in the past. You think of ways that you have handled similar problems in the past. Sometimes this is successful, but when you are faced with a new problem or when your solutions have failed, you may find it difficult to generate new ideas.

If you have a problem that seems to have no solution, try these ideas to "unfreeze" your mind:

- Relax before trying to identify alternatives.
- Play "what if" games with the problem. For example, What if money was no object? What if we could organize a festival? What if we could change winter into summer?

- Borrow ideas from other places and companies. Trade magazines might be useful in identifying approaches used by other companies.
- Give yourself permission to think of ideas that seem foolish or that appear to break the rules. For example, new recipes may come about because someone thought of new ways to combine foods. Sometimes these new combinations appear to break rules about complementary tastes or break boundaries between cuisines from different parts of the world. The results of such thinking include the combined bar and laundromat and the coffee places with Internet access for customers.
- Use random inputs to generate new ideas. For example, walk through the local shopping mall trying to find ways to apply everything you see to the problem.
- Turn the problem upside down. Can the problem be seen as an opportunity? For example, the road outside your restaurant that is the only means of accessing your parking lot is being closed due to a

bicycle race. Perhaps you could see the bicycle race as an opportunity for business rather than as a problem.

# HOW TO BE AN EFFECTIVE PROBLEM SOLVER

Every day, we all use our initiative and originality to solve problems. You might have to alter your route as a result of traffic congestion, resolve an IT issue, or determine what to make for dinner with the leftover ingredients. Although the challenges you face in your professional life are likely to be a little bit more complex than those in these examples, the methods and skills you use to solve them are largely the same because they depend on your ability to evaluate the situation and select a course of action.

Problem solving and decision making are likely essential parts of a graduate-level job, so it's important to show a recruiter that you can handle challenges, see problems as opportunities, make the right decisions, and grow from your mistakes.

In a variety of work settings, you are likely to be required to use problem-solving strategies on a daily basis, such as:

using your degree subject knowledge to resolve technical or practical issues

diagnosing and rectifying obstacles relating to processes or systems

thinking of new or different ways of doing your job

dealing with emergencies involving systems or people.

In some situations, you might need to think logically and methodically, while in others, you might need to be ready to think creatively or laterally; To find practical or technical solutions, you'll need to be able to use your academic or subject knowledge; To influence change, you will need to use other skills like communication and planning and organizing.

Regardless of the problem you're facing, the following steps are essential:

**I - Identify** the problem

**D - Define** the problem

**E - Examine** alternatives

**A - Act** on a plan

**L - Look** at the consequences

This is the **IDEAL** model of problem-solving. There are other, more complex methods, but the steps are broadly similar.

# CHAPTER 6

# 7 KEY STEPS TO IMPROVE YOUR PROBLEM SOLVING SKILLS

But everyone is born with the ability to solve problems. However, the degree to which the issue is being resolved effectively is what matters. To become the ultimate problem solver, you should therefore develop problem-solving skills. You are going to learn seven effective steps that will help you improve your ability to solve problems in this article. Let's investigate further without further ado.

## STEP 1: DEFINE THE PROBLEM

When looking for a solution to a problem, the first step is to identify and define it. You cannot proceed further unless you are aware of the issue. Therefore, you should have a solid understanding of the issue that you are going to solve. Make the problem clear and precise. Since you won't be working alone, describe the context and ensure that others involved in the decision-making process can comprehend it. However, you should keep in mind that different people have different ideas about what a problem is.

# STEP 2: ANALYSE THE PROBLEM

Analyzing a problem is the second step in solving it. It helps you comprehend the nature of the issue and locate potential solutions. At this stage, come up with creative questions for solving problems, such as "why it is a problem, why it is necessary to solve it, how to find the solution," "what barriers and opportunities lie within the problem," "what effect it will cause if the problem is not resolved," and so on.

Create these inquiries and assign responses to them. You will get a clear picture of the whole situation at the end.

This will assist you in developing your approach to resolving the issue.

# STEP 3: DEVELOP POTENTIAL SOLUTIONS

After you have finished analyzing the issue, you must look for potential solutions. Keep in mind that I said solutions rather than a solution. Finding multiple viable solutions to a problem is crucial. because you are not yet aware of the consequences of the action. Because of this, you should have options for solving the problem in every possible way so that you can compare them and choose the best one.

In this regard, you must establish a benchmark against which you will compare the potential solutions' expected outcomes. However, instead of using the standard to evaluate the solutions, use it only to generate concepts.

# STEP 4: EVALUATE THE OPTIONS

After you have finished analyzing the issue, you must look for potential solutions. Keep in mind that I said solutions rather than a solution. Finding multiple viable solutions to a problem is crucial. because you are not yet aware of the consequences of the action. Because of this, you should have options for solving the problem in every possible way so that you can compare them and choose the best one.

In this regard, you must establish a benchmark against which you will compare the potential solutions' expected outcomes. However, instead of using the standard to evaluate the solutions, use it only to generate concepts.

- Is the solution easily achievable?

- How much effort and resources it will take?

- Does it fit the organizational processes and cultures?

- What are the pros and cons of the solution?

- What is the possible outcome of this solution?

- Is it well suited to the time and budget?

Prepare the answers for each of the options and compare them. Then eliminate those which don't pass the criteria and tailor the list for further action.

# STEP 5: SELECT THE BEST OPTION

After you have finished analyzing the issue, you must look for potential solutions. Keep in mind that I said solutions rather than a solution. Finding multiple viable solutions to a problem is crucial. because you are not yet aware of the consequences of the action. Because of this, you should have options for solving the problem in every possible way so that you can compare them and choose the best one.

In this regard, you must establish a benchmark against which you will compare the potential solutions' expected outcomes. However, instead of using the standard to evaluate the solutions, use it only to generate concepts.

# STEP 6: IMPLEMENT THE SOLUTION

After you have finished analyzing the issue, you must look for potential solutions. Keep in mind that I said solutions rather than a solution. Finding multiple viable solutions to a problem is crucial. because you are not yet aware of the consequences of the action. Because of this, you should have options for solving the problem in every possible way so that you can compare them and choose the best one.

In this regard, you must establish a benchmark against which you will compare the potential solutions' expected outcomes. However, instead of using the standard to evaluate the solutions, use it only to generate concepts.

# STEP 7: MEASURE THE RESULTS

The implementation of your solution is only the beginning of your responsibility. To measure the results and ensure that the plan is effectively solving the issue, you must keep track. Great leaders always keep proper records of their actions and follow-ups. It serves as a model for their successors and is helpful for their challenges in the future. In addition, it will assist you in demonstrating to the authority a measurable and scalable outcome of your plan.

# CHAPTER 7

# CONCLUSION

It's time to come to an end. If you follow these seven easy steps, you will improve your ability to solve problems and become an effective problem solver for your company. However, there are far too many aspects of problem-solving to cover in a single article, and the subject itself is vast. Training in this area will be beneficial if you want to expand your horizons and improve your ability to solve problems.

But if you have a lot of responsibilities, how can you attend formal training? In this instance, you might want to consider enrolling in online training, which allows you to learn at any time, from any location, and, most importantly, without interfering with your regular schedule. In this regard, Training Express is providing an online course with expert instruction on problem-solving skills. Therefore, what are you awaiting? Pay attention to this.